THAT'S LIFE
PictureStories

BOOK 8
Mr. & Ms.

Tana Reiff

LAKE EDUCATION
Belmont, California

Cover Design: Ina McInnis
Text Designer: Diann Abbott

Library of Congress Catalog
Number: 94-079116

ISBN 1-56103-783-4

Printed in the United States
of America

1 9 8 7 6 5 4 3 2 1

The Marcianos

■ Frank Marciano *He owns a grocery store and has something to say on every subject.*

■ Marge Marciano *She listens to everyone's problems and knows how to help.*

■ Ernesto Marciano *Frank's father retires from life until he meets Rosa Esteban.*

■ Gina Marciano *The Marcianos' daughter is very much her own woman.*

■ Doug Kelly *He and Gina Marciano have a life plan that works for them.*

The Adamses

■ Walter Adams *Keeping up with a growing family has its problems.*

■ Ruth Adams *She manages to keep her cool through all of life's surprises.*

■ Pat Adams *A 13-year-old learns something new about life every day.*

■ Tyrone Adams *At 16, does "Mr. Basketball" really know it all?*

The Estebans

■ Carlos Esteban *Since his wife's death, he's both father and mother to his children.*

■ Rosa Esteban *Carlos's mother doesn't let age stand in the way of happiness.*

■ Rick Esteban *He finds that it's easy to get in trouble when you're 16.*

■ Roberto Esteban *This 14-year-old boy is making big plans for his future.*

■ Bonita Esteban *Growing up means having to learn about all sides of life.*

The Nguyens

■ Nguyen Lan *She can handle being a single parent in a new country.*

■ Nguyen Tam *At 4, he asks his mother why he has no father at home.*

Letters bring smiles

It's junk mail day for Don Kaufman, the mail carrier. Today he must deliver advertisements and sales letters. He says that if you don't want junk mail, just write "not accepted" on it. Then the U.S. Postal Service will send it back.

Kaufman doesn't like delivering junk mail, but he does like delivering letters. He just delivered a letter to Frank Marciano. It was from Frank's daughter, Gina. It sure made Frank happy!

What kind of mail do you like to get?

Gina's letter makes a big hit with Frank

Frank Marciano has just read the letter from Gina. He is so excited that Marge wonders if her husband is all right. Their neighbor Ruth Adams asks if Frank got money in the mail.

"Better than that!" shouts Frank. He says that he has big news. But Marge isn't excited. She knows that Frank can sometimes get excited over nothing.

What do you think the big news might be?

Gina's big surprise

Finally, Frank tells everybody the news.

"You know how Gina left home seven years ago?" Frank asks. He makes it sound as if Gina ran away from home. But she only went away to school. Then she got a job in another town. Now she and her friend Doug Kelly are moving back to town. Gina already has a new job.

When was the last time you got exciting news in the mail? What was it?

Gina kept her secret well

Marge is surprised at the news. Gina hadn't even told them that she was looking for a job in town. She wanted to surprise her parents.

"But Gina was never able to keep a secret!" laughs Marge. That makes it even more of a surprise!

Gina's letter says that she will be home "in a few minutes." Ruth thinks that it must be a mistake. Gina must have wanted to say "months" instead of "minutes."

Is it difficult for you to keep a secret?

It must be Frank's lucky day

Hello? Gina! Where are you? Across the street at Michael's Pub? No wonder you said, "in a few minutes!" We'll be right there.

Store's closed! Let's go. Ruth, come with us.

No, you 2 go. I'll see you later.

Suddenly the telephone rings and Frank answers it. It's Gina! She is across the street at Michael's Pub. When she had said "in a few minutes" in her letter, she was right. Frank tells her that they will be right over. He closes the store and invites Ruth to come along.

"No," says Ruth. "You two go. I'll see you later."

Why does Frank close the store?

Gina gets a warm welcome

Gina and Doug are sitting in Michael's Pub when Frank and Marge walk in.

"Mom, Dad, you remember Doug," Gina says. Marge and Frank shake hands with Doug. They have met before.

Gina has something she wants to say right away. She says that she is moving back to the area, but not back home. She wants to be sure her father understands this.

What kind of father do you think Frank is?

Gina explains her plans

Frank orders a bottle of champagne. Then he asks Gina when the big date is. He wants to know when Doug and Gina are getting married. But instead, Gina tells him that her new job starts in two weeks.

Doug is looking for a job in the building trade. They will move to town next week. They have even found a small apartment already. But Frank wants Gina to live at home. He hasn't listened to what Gina was saying. She doesn't want to live at home.

How do you know that Frank hasn't been listening to Gina?

Frank gets another surprise

"There is no date, Dad," Gina says when Frank asks again about the big date. She wants to tell her parents about her plans at another time. Gina knows that her father is getting upset.

Just then Michael brings them the champagne that Frank had ordered.

Marge thinks that she knows what Gina has to say.

"Maybe we'd better wait to talk," Marge says, looking at Frank.

Do you think it is a better idea to talk later?

Sometimes the truth hurts

Frank is getting angry. He wants Gina to tell him *now* what's going on.

"Dad," Gina begins slowly. "Doug and I are going to live together. We aren't ready to get married just yet."

Frank doesn't want to hear any more. He just can't believe what Gina is saying.

"Daddy, it's not that terrible," says Gina.

Why doesn't Frank want to hear any more?

Frank takes the news hard

Gina says that it's common now for people to live together without being married.

Frank takes the word "common" to mean "second rate," not "usual."

"It's common and *low!* Is this *your* idea, Doug?" Frank asks.

Doug stays cool. "It's the decision of two people who love each other," Doug answers Frank.

"I raised you better," Frank tells Gina.

If many people are doing something, does that mean that it's OK to do?

Frank has nothing else to say

Gina is sorry that her father is upset about her plans to live with Doug. She wants to talk to Frank alone in the park tomorrow. Maybe by then he will have cooled off.

Then Gina and Doug stand up to leave. Doug says that he's sorry about everything.

"Things will be fine, Doug," Marge says. Maybe she is planning to talk to Frank later. In any case, Marge takes the news pretty well.

Do you think that Frank will change his mind about Doug and Gina's plans?

All good things come to an end

Marge and Frank are alone now in Michael's Pub. Frank is feeling very unhappy. He doesn't understand his daughter anymore.

Then Michael comes to the table to get $17 for the champagne. Frank has to pay for it.

"First they break my heart," says Frank. "Then they stick me for the drinks!" Things couldn't be worse.

Do you think Frank has good reasons to feel the way he does?

Doug and Gina check it out

A real estate agent is showing Gina and Doug a townhouse that's for sale. They want to buy a house rather than rent an apartment. The owners of the townhouse seem to be asking a fair price.

The house is in a nice part of town, which means it costs more. Gina wonders if they can afford it.

Why do you think that Doug and Gina want to buy a house?

The down payment is a little too high

Doug and Gina will have to put money down to buy the townhouse. They will have to pay 30% of the price of the house for the down payment. But they have only $16,000 in cash for the down payment.

Gina has more money to put down than Doug. But if he does more cooking, she will call it even!

Do you think that Doug and Gina can buy this townhouse?

The agent has some ideas

The real estate agent knows that Gina and Doug don't have enough money for the down payment. But he has two ideas. If Doug or Gina had been in the armed services, he or she could get a GI loan. Then the down payment would be less. They could also borrow money from their life insurance. The insurance company would loan them some of the money they have paid for their policy.

But neither idea works for Doug and Gina.

How else might Gina and Doug get enough money for the down payment?

Gina and Doug get another chance

I really like this house. Everything checks out: good roof, new wiring, good pipes, and the furnace is in good shape.

Not all buyers check those things, but they should.

I have another townhouse almost like this one. But it is smaller and it needs some work.

Let's look at it. We could fix it up ourselves. And we don't need a big house. Let's go see it!

Gina and Doug really like this townhouse. The roof, the wiring, the pipes, and the furnace are all in good shape. If they weren't, it could cost a lot of money to have them fixed.

The agent tells them about another townhouse that's for sale. It is smaller and needs some work. So the price will be lower than this one.

Gina wants to have a look at it. She is excited. Maybe she and Doug can buy a house after all!

Would you buy a house that needs repairs?

Marge finds a chair

Marge is looking for furniture for Gina and Doug's new house.

"Isn't that a great chair?" the salesperson asks Marge.

"Yes," says Marge. "But could you help me get out of it?" Marge sinks down into the chair and can't get up.

The chair is a good buy. So Marge buys one like it in a different color.

Why do you think Marge wants to buy something for Gina and Doug?

Marge pays cash

Marge wants the store to deliver the chair. She will give the salesperson Gina and Doug's address. Then Marge pays for the chair with cash.

"Cash!" says the surprised salesperson. "We don't see that very often." He gives Marge her change and a sales receipt. If anything is wrong, Marge will have her receipt. It proves that she bought the chair from this store.

Why is it a good idea to save receipts?

Ernesto has an idea

Suddenly, Frank's father, Ernesto, comes into the store. He runs up to Marge with a big smile on his face.

"Marge!" Ernesto says. "I just found something that will help the kids get started. But I need $5."

Marge loans him $10.

Ernesto has found a book for Frank. It will give Frank something to think about besides Gina and Doug!

Will it help Gina if Frank gets interested in something else?

A heart-to-heart talk

Frank and Gina are in the park together, talking. Frank is still feeling bad about Gina living with Doug.

"Why don't you just get married?" Frank asks Gina.

Gina explains that they aren't ready to get married yet. But they love each other now and are happy together. Someday, she and Doug might get married—but not now.

Who do you think places more importance on marriage—Frank or Gina?

Gina doesn't agree

Frank thinks that only marriage gives a woman and a man the right to live together. But Gina doesn't agree. She thinks that a piece of paper that says you're married is not as important as love.

Frank is worried about what people will think of his daughter. But he doesn't want her to leave town.

How much do you think people should care about what others think of them?

Gina has changed

Frank still thinks of Gina as his little girl. But she is 25 now. She has grown up a lot since she lived at home.

"I have to be my own woman," Gina says. She must do what she thinks is right. Frank can no longer make her decisions for her.

How are Frank and Gina alike?

Kaufman knows what's going on

Kaufman brings us up-to-date on the story. Frank was glad that his daughter Gina and her friend Doug were going to live in town. But he wasn't happy for very long. Gina and Doug told him that they were buying a house and moving in together. And they're not getting married!

Frank tried to talk them out of it, but Gina has to live her own life. Marge took the news well. She even bought them some new furniture for their house.

What would make Frank happy?

Walter Adams has his own ideas

Frank and his neighbor Walter Adams are building shelves at Marge and Frank's store. They are talking about Frank's problem with Gina. Frank tells Walter that no one knows what's right anymore. Frank thinks that it's only right that Gina and Doug get married.

"Things are changing," Walter says. He tells Frank that young people today look at things in a different way. If Frank doesn't accept Gina's decision, he could lose her.

Do you think that Walter would feel the same way if Gina were his daughter?

Walter knows how it is

Walter tries to help Frank with his problem. Walter remembers being upset when he and his wife were going to have their third baby. If he had stayed cool, he could have saved himself a lot of trouble. He says that if Frank would accept things as they are, he would feel a lot better.

Frank might be able to accept Gina, but Doug is another story.

Do you agree with what Walter says?

Frank worries too much

Frank thinks that if Gina and Doug would get married, it would solve a lot of problems. Then the money they earn would be *theirs*—not his and hers. They would own everything together. Everything will get mixed up if they aren't married. So Frank thinks that when they break up, they will come to him for help.

"That's one thing you don't have to worry about!" jokes Walter.

Do you think Frank would help Gina if she asked him?

Living together is a partnership agreement

Gina and Doug are in a lawyer's office. Since they are buying a house together, the lawyer wants them to make a written partnership agreement. This way, all the details of what each person owns will be in writing. If Gina and Doug ever break up, it will be easier to divide everything.

Do you think a partnership agreement is a good idea?

Keeping track

The lawyer will write down all the things that Doug and Gina agree on. And he wants them to keep track of the money they spend together, especially on the house. This way, they will know just who owns what.

If Gina spends more money on the house, then she will get more money when they sell the house. But Doug and Gina will have to keep a careful record of who paid what.

Should married people also make a written agreement?

Planning ahead

Doug and Gina will write down what each one spends on house payments, house repairs, gas and electricity, and furniture. Every month they will add up the money each one spent on the house.

The lawyer will also help them work out a plan for selling the house. Doug and Gina want to be fair with each other.

Is it easy to keep track of the money you spend?

3 for dinner

"Do I get to come to dinner in your new house?" the lawyer asks, before Gina and Doug leave the office.

Doug would rather eat at the lawyer's house. Neither he nor Gina is a very good cook. But Gina wants to go to a restaurant. That idea is fine with the lawyer, if everyone shares the cost of the meal. That's how a partnership agreement works!

What does "Dutch treat" mean?

Kaufman plays the waiting game

Kaufman checks his own mailbox. He is waiting to hear from a publisher about publishing his book. But there is no letter for him today.

"It's hard to wait sometimes," Kaufman says. He knows something else that is difficult. When you buy something and have trouble with it, it can be difficult to get the store to fix the problem. That's what Marge is doing now.

"Whatever happened to the days when the customer was always right?" Marge had said to Kaufman.

Do you believe that "the customer is always right"?

The store made a mistake

Marge and Gina are at the furniture store. Marge is upset because the store delivered the wrong chair. And the salesperson is not being helpful. He wants Marge and Gina to return the chair themselves. After that, the store will deliver the one Marge wants.

"What do you want me to do?" shouts Marge. "*Carry* it?"

"I'm sure the gentleman will take care of this," Gina says, trying to calm her mother.

Would a salesperson be more willing to help an angry or a calm person?

A bad idea

"Maybe you could use a truck to return the chair," says the salesperson.

"I don't own a truck!" shouts Marge. Renting a truck can cost $45 or $50. Marge would also have to pay mileage. The salesperson says that Marge and Gina could share the cost.

If you were Marge, would you rent a truck to take the chair back to the store?

Enough is enough!

Gina asks to talk to the store manager. She has had enough of the salesperson. But Ms. Washington is out of town. The salesperson reminds them of the company contract. It says that the store will give them the chair they want when they return the other one.

"I should sue you," says Marge. If she takes this problem to court, Marge thinks she would have a good case.

Do you think that Marge would have a good case in court?

The Marcianos aren't done yet

"Go ahead and sue!" says the salesperson. "Going to court will cost you a lot of money. It would cost a lot less to rent a truck."

Gina tells him about small claims court. This is a low-cost way to sue. It doesn't cost much to present a case, and you don't need a lawyer.

"We're going to return that chair," says Gina, "and then we'll see you in court!"

If you were Marge, would you be angry with the salesperson?

Today it goes back

Doug and Frank are going to take the chair back to the store. Frank has rented a trailer and hitched it to his car. He and Doug go inside the house to get the chair.

"There's nothing wrong with that chair," says Frank. It's true that there is nothing wrong with the chair itself. But the chair is purple and the rug is red. The colors just don't go well together.

Do you think that Frank is trying to get along with Doug?

Frank knows better

Frank thinks that the chair looks fine, but he won't argue about it. After 30 years with Marge, he knows better. He always loses.

"You've been married 30 years?" asks Doug.

"It's too bad we'll never be able to say the same for you and Gina," Frank says. He is still upset that Gina and Doug are living together without being married.

If you were Doug, how would you feel about Frank at this point?

Frank has some questions

Frank is still not used to the idea of Doug and Gina living together without being married. He wants to know if they will have children "that way." And what would their children's last names be?

Doug and Gina aren't planning to have children right now. But when they do, the children might have both last names—Marciano-Kelly. Frank thinks that is a terrible idea!

Why doesn't Frank like the name Marciano-Kelly?

A woman with a cause

Marge will sue the furniture store in small claims court. Frank will go to court with her, Gina, and Doug. He knows that Marge will fight for her rights. He calls her a "housewife with a cause."

"You mean home manager," Doug says. That is a better name to describe the job of a person who takes care of a home. (But, of course, Marge works in the store, too, just like Frank.) The job of home manager is worth at least $14,000 a year.

How much money do you think the job of home manager is worth?

It isn't Frank's lucky day

Frank has trouble thinking of Marge as a "home manager" and not as a "housewife." "Home manager" makes him think of a liberated woman. Frank does not agree with Doug about liberated women. He has a different idea about what those words mean.

Frank just wants to get the chair downtown now. He starts the car and drives away. Suddenly there is a loud crash.

"Oh, no!" screams Frank. "The trailer came off!" It's another one of those difficult days.

Why do you think the trailer came off?

Kaufman and Marge keep pushing on

Kaufman just got some bad news. The publisher doesn't want his book. So Kaufman will send his book to another publisher. He will keep trying.

And Marge will keep trying to get the furniture store to pay for its mistake. She is taking the store manager to small claims court. Marge will be her own lawyer there.

What kind of person is Marge Marciano?

Marge tells it like it is

Marge stands up in court to present her case.

"I told the salesperson that I didn't want the chair in the showroom. It was the wrong color. I explained that it wouldn't go well with the rug," Marge tells the judge.

"Marge has very good taste," Frank breaks in.

Marge explains that the problem started when the store delivered the wrong chair.

Do you think Marge is presenting her case well?

The store manager has her say

Next the store manager tells her side of the story.

"I told Mrs. Marciano that we'd take the chair back and give her another one," says the manager. "People like her are not reasonable. They cause prices to go up."

"And people like you give business a bad name," Frank breaks in again.

"Please, Mr. Marciano," the judge says to Frank.

What is another way a business might get a bad name?

Reading between the lines

The store manager explains the store's contract that Marge signed. The contract says that the *buyer* must return the product. After that, the buyer can get the money returned or get the right product.

"People don't read contracts!" shouts the manager. Besides, she says, it's no problem to return things.

"But why would I pay for your mistake?" asks Marge. Marge is staying cool, but Frank is not. He breaks in again.

Do you read the contracts that you sign?

The case is closed

Marge says that she has tried to be fair. She wants the store to pay for the trailer rental. And she also wants $100 for her trouble. Then the store manager brings up the contract again. But the judge has heard enough.

He decides that the store should pay for the cost of the trailer. The store's contract wasn't fair to Marge—because the store made the mistake. But the judge won't let Marge have the extra $100. With that, the case is closed.

How would you have decided the case if you were the judge?

Frank and Marge are quite a couple

Frank still wants Doug and Gina to get married. He will keep trying to talk them into it. He just never gives up.

When Doug and Gina go to get the car, Frank puts his arm around Marge.

"I was real proud of you," Frank says to Marge. "You're quite a woman."

Marge smiles. She thinks Frank is pretty special himself.

Why is Frank proud of Marge?